To Mikey - for your birthday
in 1995. Aren't all really
good things worth waiting
for.?!
Ever- loving,
Chunky.
24. 3. 97.

SNOWDON ON STAGE

SNOWDON ON STAGE

WITH A PERSONAL VIEW OF THE BRITISH THEATRE 1954–1996

BY SIMON CALLOW

PAVILION

First published in Great Britain in 1996 by
PAVILION BOOKS LIMITED
26 Upper Ground, London SE1 9PD

Photographs copyright © Snowdon 1996
Introduction copyright © Simon Callow 1996
Captions copyright © Snowdon 1996
The caption dates refer to the year the photograph was taken.

Designed by Price Watkins Design

The moral right of the author has been asserted.

A CIP catalogue record of this book is available from the British Library

ISBN 1 85793 919 0 (hbk)
ISBN 1 86205 040 6 (pbk)

Typeset in Frutiger light
Printed and bound in Spain by Bookprint

2 4 6 8 10 9 7 5 3 1

This book may be ordered by post direct from the publisher.
Please contact the marketing department.
But try your bookshop first.

To my dear grandson

Sam

A personal view of the British theatre 1954–1996
BY SIMON CALLOW

50s

TONY ARMSTRONG JONES (as Snowdon then was) started photographing for the theatre in what might be called the immediately pre-revolutionary period, just before the bomb that realigned the theatrical landscape went off with the premiere of John Osborne's *Look Back in Anger* at the Royal Court in 1956.

About time too, say the books. The fifties are firmly established in folklore as a period of benighted frivolity during which the British theatre spinelessly complied with the demand of Kenneth Tynan's mythical Aunt Edna for perfect tastefulness and complete absence of content. It is now apparent, from the perspective of the overinflated and undernourished theatre of the nineties, that it was instead a peculiarly rich period, enviably audacious and abundant. From this angle, the *ancien régime* of 1954 (the year of Tony Armstrong Jones's first assignment) was providing the theatre-going population with rich and stimulating fare, if in a manner perhaps a little too self-congratulatory for comfort.

It was another world from ours: no National Theatre, no Royal Shakespeare Company, no fringe; the Royal Court a neglected playhouse on Sloane Square with a glorious past rather far behind it. Every summer in Stratford-upon-Avon, the Shakespeare Memorial Theatre staged a season of plays led by the great actors of the day (who included Michael Redgrave, Laurence Olivier, Edith Evans, Peggy Ashcroft, John Gielgud and Ralph Richardson), while the Old Vic Company, with occasional visits from some of these luminaries, sometimes creating luminaries of its own like John Neville and Richard Burton, was slowly working its way through the entire canon, maintaining as best it could on an exiguous budget the great tradition of popular classical theatre established there by Lilian Baylis; while the tiny Arts Theatre hard by Leicester Square tube station pursued an enterprising policy, first under Alec Clunes (a great Shaw cycle), then under a baby-faced but fiercely determined Peter Hall, who had just directed the English-language premiere of Beckett's *Waiting for Godot* there, a piece generally considered to be unplayable and incomprehensible, but almost immediately afterwards understood to be a key work of both the modern age and the modern stage. It established Hall, at the age of twenty-six, in a central position in the British theatre from which he never retreated.

Outside the centre of London, most suburbs had touring theatres; many had producing theatres. Throughout the country, from Land's End in the West Country to Wick in the extreme north of Scotland, every city, every *town*, had its own repertory theatre, and most of them maintained regular companies, which kept together for a year or even two. First on the road, then with Theatre Workshop at Stratford in the East End of London, Joan Littlewood, was, with her violent hatred of cultural piety, taking the classics by the scruff of their necks and shaking them like rats, till they seemed like new plays. At the other end of the theatrical spectrum, but equally contemptuous of polished production values, Donald Wolfit and his touring company roamed the land like a ragged army of thespian Visigoths, shaking the rafters of whichever halfway adequate building it could hire for the least possible outlay, occasionally foraying into far-flung parts of the metropolis, where astonished theatregoers could witness the continuing vigorous survival of a tradition that seemed to hark back to the medieval strolling players and beyond.

For the rest, it was the West End of London, the largest concentration of theatres in the world, which was dominated by the taste and judgement of one man, the producer Hugh 'Binkie' Beaumont, of H.M. Tennent Ltd. There were other producers, of course, many of them, producing revues, saucy comedies, thrillers, straight plays; certain theatres, like the Whitehall under the farceur Brian Rix, were identified with a particular genre. But it was Binkie who set the tone; he occupied, indeed defined, the high theatrical ground. Weaving a web of influence and financial inducements, Binkie siphoned off the cream – the best acting, the best design, the best new writing on both sides of the Atlantic and either side of the Channel. Anouilh, Giraudoux, Sartre, leaders of the theatrical avant-garde, were staple West End fare during the fifties.

Binkie was above all a master of what would now be called packaging, putting together the most appropriate team for the work in hand. In effect he maintained a floating company whose members formed the élite of the profession; an actor-manager like Laurence Olivier remained outside of his net, but the concentration of talent in his shows remains astonishing. He had strong and admirable instincts concerning both production (as it was then called) and design. Among the directors whom he most frequently employed was Peter Brook, still, at twenty-nine, a *wünderkind*, but already an absolute master of every known form of theatre – classical, boulevard, realistic, symbolic, musical comedy, opera. Before long, he would be drawn to exploring the *unk*nown forms of theatre, but for the rest of the decade, he was a happily inescapable feature of West End theatre, creating ravishingly orchestrated and dazzlingly staged production after production, which taken together represent the *apogée* of commercial theatre in our time; the season he directed at the Phoenix Theatre consisting of *The Family Reunion*, *Hamlet* and an adaptation of Graham Greene's *The Power and the Glory* counts as the crowning glory of the post-war West End, all three plays starring his protégé Paul Scofield supported by an astonishing group of fellow players including Sybil Thorndike and Gwen Ffrangçon-Davis.

It must have seemed that things would go on like this forever, simply getting better and better – new Scofields and new Brooks would arise and take over and the feast would never end. In fact, it was to prove the final flowering of the West End as a creative centre, though it was several years before that fact became clear. Society had changed in critical ways; the immediately post-war consensus was beginning to collapse, and the illusion of a country unified across class and national divides was breaking down, while feeble post-Imperial shenanigans made clear Britain's decline as an international power. The theatre, seemingly always several steps behind overt social change, had begun to chafe at what seemed an ineluctable middle-class domination of the medium – not merely in the new plays presented, which seemed to address themselves exclusively to the concerns of the well-heeled Home Counties, but equally in the plush, upholstered production values encouraged by Binkie and his coevals.

This applied equally to the acting style of what is generally referred to as the last great generation of British actors. An important condition for the theatrical revolution had been inaugurated with the appointment of John Fernald as Principal of the Royal Academy of Dramatic Art. His programme was to transform the school's image as a sort of glorified finishing school in which students' rough edges were smoothed down till they conformed to the norms of BBC English and the manners of Mayfair. Accordingly, he encouraged actors from the regions to retain both their accents and their energy. When new forms of theatre were attempted, there was thus a new generation of actors ready and able to realize them.

The younger directors and writers, meanwhile, had been agitating with increasing vehemence both for a theatre that would better reflect life in modern Britain, and for a more serious commitment from the state to the idea of the theatre. This move crystallized in the dream of a National Theatre, a dream which had been maintained, fruitlessly, for over a century. Lip service had recently been paid to the idea. Foundation stones had been laid, but no building had taken place. The revolution finally started, as they so often do, quietly enough, with the creation at the Royal Court of the English Stage Company by George Devine, an actor, teacher and director of Olivier's generation, assisted by Tony Richardson, the epitome of the new generation of directors, from Bradford via Oxford, restlessly determined to inherit the kingdom of the theatre, but on his terms. The company was dedicated, from the outset, to the encouragement of new playwrights: its subtitle, never abandoned, was the Writer's Theatre.

The writers they actually had in mind at first were novelists, so much more in touch with modern life, it seemed, than contemporary playwrights; and the first season accordingly consisted of plays by writers such as Angus Wilson and Nigel Dennis who had never written one before. Included among the work of these novelists was an original play by an actor who was a member of the company. This play, in many ways quite old-fashioned in its technique, by expressing a voice unheard for many years either in the drawing-room or on the stage – passionate, rhetorical, and denunciatory – became the rallying point for a whole generation who were champing for a braver, newer world, both in theatre and in life. Its merits as a play were secondary to its embodiment of this voice; its very title – *Look Back in Anger* – became the slogan of a generation. Its author, John Osborne, later said of the theatre that it was a minority art with a majority influence. His play convinced people who would never have dreamt of going into a playhouse that the theatre had something important to say to them, and to England.

This was Tony Armstrong Jones's hour. An unlikely revolutionary, his witty restlessness wanted change too. He was more or less born into the theatrical purple. His uncle, Oliver Messel, was the dominant figure in English theatre design for over four decades, supreme in revue, musical comedy, ballet and opera, but equally at home in Shakespeare; his experience ranged from Cochran in the twenties to Brook, again and again, in the fifties. Armstrong Jones had been close to Messel from childhood, even being allowed to work on the masks for one of the later Cochran revues. It was through Messel that Armstrong Jones was introduced to the powerful director Peter Glenville, then in the throes of staging Terence Rattigan's *Separate Tables* with those two superb actors Margaret Leighton and Eric Portman. Glenville invited the young photographer (whose greatest triumph up to that point had been – moonshining from his work as assistant to the society photographer Baron – covering one of Messel's parties for *Picture Post* in 1953) to do the production photographs.

This he did, according to the usual practice of the day. At a specially staged session, he was free to rearrange the furniture and, indeed, the actors to create an appropriate image, which would then be brought to a level of artificial perfection by a range of subtle re-touching refinements. The leading theatrical photographers of the time, the classically simple Houston Rogers and the rather more fantastical Angus McBean, were masters of this technique, for which, shrouded in the traditional black cloth, they employed plate cameras, mentally righting the inverted image they saw through the ground glass. Armstrong Jones, impatient with the rigidity and complexity of this method, longed to photograph an actual performance, or indeed a rehearsal, with a camera which could respond quickly to what he saw. Photographing *Separate Tables* he managed to vary the procedure by going backstage with a miniature camera to snap the actors as they made up, and experimented with double exposure of the two parts played by Margaret Leighton in the same frame, but otherwise dutifully provided the standard front-of-house photographs; all the time, though, his natural instinct for impressionism was at war with the style they represented. The control and conscious artistry of those photographs was the opposite of what he wanted; temperamentally and as a matter of photographic philosophy he believed in snaps, not studies. He wanted, in his own words, to 'sum up a moment more than that moment . . . to pin down a style or an attitude'. His deeply engrained theatricality was less to do with the artifice of the event than with its actuality and its evanescence.

For this purpose, the smooth, perfectly lit, perfectly focused surfaces favoured by certain old-fashioned managements were less immediate than the 'wrong' – 'ugly' – photographic style favoured by newsdesks but rejected as grainy and out of focus by the theatre page. He welcomed, even courted, accidents which often conveyed the impact of a performance more vividly than what he had planned to take. Finding himself too far away from the stage at an under-lit run-through of another Peter Glenville production, *Hotel Paradiso*, he ended up with a dim and grainy image, not even in costume, of Alec Guinness's virtuoso farce performance. Taking a detail, he blew it up and bleached out the eyes with potassium ferrocyanide. This startling image he then put outside the theatre as part of the front-of-house display. Soon he was in universal demand and – much encouraged by the producer Toby Rowland – set about adorning the façades of London's theatres with huge blow-ups, to get people, as he said, 'off the buses and into the theatres'. The theatre critic of the *Daily Express*, John Barber, was so stunned by the image from *Hotel Paradiso*, and its vivid account of Guinness's performance, that he surreptitiously took it down after the first night and gave it to his editor, who immediately printed it, to the outrage of Armstrong Jones's own editor at the *Weekly Sketch* who had paid £2 for exclusive rights. Harold Keeble at the *Express*, creator of the famous *Photonews* feature, became Armstrong Jones's greatest patron; together they literally made the theatre into news.

The photographic revolution was not to everyone's taste. The immensely distinguished actress Gwen Ffrangçon-Davis was sighted on a small pair of stepladders outside a Shaftesbury Avenue theatre tearing down the front-of-house photograph Armstrong Jones had taken of her, and replacing it with one by Angus McBean. 'I don't want my photographs to look like me-in-the-play,' she complained, 'I want them to look like me.' She was fighting a rearguard action. The West End of 1955 desperately wanted to be exciting, modern, new. Directors, moreover, were delighted not to have to endure the long and tedious photocalls that previous styles entailed, as were most actors, from the majority of whom Armstrong Jones received warm co-operation: 'Olivier turned to me and asked me what I would like him to do, and I was suddenly in the terrifying position of directing Olivier.' Armstrong Jones's irresistible personal charm, at once vulnerable and commanding, sometimes provocatively capricious but always fascinating, creates an event out of a sitting; no danger of boredom there. Actors gave their best performances for his camera.

Armstrong Jones was not merely outside the theatres. On one striking occasion, he was actually on stage; or at least his work was. John Cranko, the brilliantly daring South African ex-Royal Ballet choreographer, had invited him to design the revue *Keep Your Hair On*. He did so with an entirely characteristic combination of huge grainy photographic blow-ups – the first time this had been done in the theatre, unmistakably his work, and unmistakably contemporary – and (in his words) 'extremely complicated mechanical and electrical gadgets'. He is happiest in his workshop rather than in his darkroom, designing and making anything from furniture to optical clocks to the Chairmobile (a motorized platform – small enough to go in the back of a Mini – for disabled people) to the gigantic walk-through aviary at London Zoo, the largest tension structure of its kind, built in 1963 and now a listed building. Curiously enough, except for the odd light, he has not been at all interested in the technicalities of photography, wanting above all to avoid self-consciousness in either photographer or subject.

In the event, *Keep Your Hair On* was a disaster, a famous one, though the sets were acclaimed as new and fascinating. This did not stop him, on the first night, from throwing up in the men's room from sheer nerves; one of the reasons he has such sympathy with actors is that he has been in their boots. He never designed a show again. Theatrical disasters notwithstanding, Armstrong Jones had become, in a very short space of time, one of the defining personalities of his time. His new photographic look was the perfect medium with which to record the sixties butterfly as it emerged from its fifties chrysalis. His work in the theatre records the transition, across a range of writers new and old – T. S. Eliot (a highly successful West End dramatist as well as High Priest of the modern poetic movement) and W. Somerset Maugham (yesterday's playwright, or the day before yesterday's, a man of the theatre of the 'teens, twenties and thirties); John Osborne, John Arden, Arnold Wesker and Peter Shaffer on the brink of their tremendous careers; Brendan Behan representing Joan Littlewood's hotbed of theatrical innovation at the Theatre Workshop, utterly anti-establishment, more profoundly so than the Royal Court because really rooted in working-class experience; Anouilh, still, for a brief moment longer, both fashionable and intellectually respectable – and an equally wide range of actors, from Michael Redgrave and Barbara Jefford at their noblest and most articulate in Giraudoux's *Tiger at the Gates*, Dirk Bogarde and Geraldine McEwan enacting love's young dream in *Summertime*, daringly photographed away from the theatre, on location in Edinburgh (another of Armstrong Jones's innovations not appreciated by the set designers); Paul Massie and Kim Stanley in Tennessee Williams's searing *Cat on a Hot Tin Roof* and Anthony Quayle and Brian Bedford in Miller's equally impassioned *View from the Bridge*, directed by Peter Brook, banned by the Lord Chamberlain on account of a kiss between two men and so played under a club licence, here photographed by Armstrong Jones down in the docks; through the great Personality Actors, even at the time an endangered species, now entirely vanished from the face of the earth: Robert Morley, Gladys Cooper, beautifully retouched as a tribute to a vanishing age, and a very young Leslie Caron (seen here both in *Gigi* and at Marylebone Road Registry Office, having just married Peter Hall – Armstrong Jones was the only witness); John Neville, the last of the *acteurs nobles*, certainly the last of that breed to attempt to play Hamlet; and Scofield, unmistakably a great classical actor, at the same time unmistakably modern; and Laurence Olivier, a colossus with a foot in two worlds of theatre.

Unlike his contemporaries, who publicly denounced the exploding new world of theatre, Olivier immediately grasped its importance and determined to be part of it. In Osborne's Archie Rice in *The Entertainer* he found a role in which he could bring to bear all the armoury of skills he had wrought in the classical theatre to create a character that embodied and defined a moment in British history, his made-up face a mask to set alongside any of the haunting masks of history, those of the *commedia dell'arte* or the tribes of Central America or Africa and the Far East. The contact sheets reproduced here give a vivid sense of aspects of his performance, while the specific cropping of the chosen frame gives the lie to anyone who thinks that photography, and particularly Snowdon's, is mere recording. There is nothing mere about the meticulous construction of such an image.

Olivier's astonishing power of transformation, both of himself and of his career (*The Entertainer* appeared at the Royal Court only two years after *Look Back in Anger* had been expected to sweep away the theatre that Olivier, more than anyone else, had represented), triumphantly endorsed the great hope of the fifties, to create a drama which said something about Britain as it really was. In the early 1960s that tremendous power harnessed itself to the other great dream of the period: the National Theatre. Not, however, before Peter Hall, who had steadily been consolidating his theatrical base, transformed the seasonal Stratford Memorial Theatre into a permanent ensemble, with a distinct and recognizable style of its own, and a London home at the Aldwych Theatre. This newly christened Royal Shakespeare Company would mingle new work with an approach to Shakespeare which directly referred to the present age; *Shakespeare Our Contemporary*, the title of Jan Kott's influential book, was the watchword. The first seasons included a *Hamlet* with a student rebel Prince in the form of David Warner, and, perhaps the most significant single production of the decade, the *Wars of the Roses* (comprising and compressing *Henry IV*, *V* and *VI*), which built a bridge between the two Elizabethan ages, ours and Shakespeare's; a number of the most powerful new plays of the epoch, from both Europe and America, were included in the Aldwych repertory.

The new realism established at the Royal Court was a palpable influence on the Company's playing style, as was the increasing impact of Bertolt Brecht, whose political position, which many of the younger generation of writers and directors shared, seemed perfectly mirrored in the aesthetic he had evolved for his Berliner Ensemble; their first visit to London in 1956 cast, for better and for worse, a long shadow over the British theatre that only disappeared in the early eighties. Peter Brook, in his radical productions for the company of *The Physicists*, *King Lear* (with Scofield), *US* and *The Assassination and Persecution of Marat as Performed under the Direction of the Marquis De Sade* showed how far he had moved from the dappled and enchanted world of *Ring Round the Moon* of only a decade before. Peter Hall's work was always more textually orientated than Brook's intensely physicalized universe. At the core of his company were actors of a deeply serious bent, Eric Porter, Ian Holm and – above all – the great actress Peggy Ashcroft, Juliet to Olivier and Gielgud's alternating Romeo and Mercutio, Desdemona to Robeson's Othello, a rare and profound spirit, as politically radical as she was theatrically authentic; she was the rock upon whom Hall built his theatre.

Meanwhile, Olivier, using the Chichester Festival as a springboard, had finally and triumphantly – in surprising but brilliantly effective collaboration with the radical-chic critic Kenneth Tynan – established the National Theatre at the Old Vic on entirely different principles from those of the RSC. The National would espouse no company style, seeking instead to challenge itself with, and adapt itself to, the special and varying demands of the whole range of world dramatic literature, no less, from which the repertory was to be drawn. To this end, a succession of the world's greatest stage directors were invited to mount productions in Lilian Baylis's old theatre in the Waterloo Road, which they did, with dazzling results; at the same time a retrospective of neglected British plays was mounted (*Trelawny of the Wells* and Nöel Coward's *Hay Fever*, initiating Coward's recall from critical oblivion); while a roster of young directors, many drawn from the Royal Court, kept up the end of the new drama (John Arden, Peter Shaffer, and the dazzling new verbal pyrotechnician, Tom Stoppard) while challenging assumptions about the classics. William Gaskill's productions, for example, reinventing the entire tradition of playing Restoration and post-Restoration comedy.

With the great continental companies as their ideal, Olivier and Tynan, like Peter Hall, determined to create a permanent ensemble. The National's company was drawn from a potent mix of classical actors (Michael Redgrave and Edith Evans), West End stars (Maggie Smith, for example, and the veteran Max Adrian), and raw, hungry young actors, many from the Royal Court (Robert Stephens, Frank Finlay, Colin Blakely, Ian McKellen). The reps were combed for the boldest and most colourful of young hopefuls, whose numbers included Derek Jacobi, Michael Gambon and Anthony Hopkins, all carrying their proverbial spears – but not for long, for the essential principle of building company strength from within was scrupulously maintained. At the centre of things was the matchlessly glamorous and inspiring figure of Olivier himself, at the peak of his immense physical powers, leading the company from the front in a succession of great roles: Othello, Uncle Vanya, Edgar in *The Dance of Death*, Shylock. Colour, courage, flair and virtuosity distinguished the company's work, an unprecedented combination of intellectual adventurousness, experimentation in design, and high octane performance; this last, of course,

was the spirit of Olivier extended across an entire company. The Waterloo Road became the mecca of every theatre pilgrim.

The centre of the theatrical universe had decisively shifted; the West End seemed a genteel enclave stranded in history beside the huge theatrical outpouring represented by the RSC (at Stratford, the Aldwych and, more experimentally, at the Arts), the National (which soon created the Young Vic, in a converted butcher's shop down the road from the Vic) and the Royal Court, which, since George Devine's death, had become more radical; here Edward Bond, perhaps, with Pinter the greatest of post-war dramatists, created a body of work which amounts to a view of modern Britain that is still terrifying in its intensity, setting the tone with *Saved* for a kind of theatre that made Osborne's rhetorical flights seem merely dyspeptic. The Lord Chamberlain's power of censorship had finally, after nearly 250 years, been abolished, and taboos were quickly abandoned one after another: nudity was allowed, as was *lèse majesté* and every kind of swearword; the Royal Court, especially, availed itself of all its new freedoms.

In the hands of its most enterprising impresarios, Michael Codron leader among them, the West End was still capable of originating daring work, for example that of Simon Gray (*Wise Child* with Alec Guinness in drag) and Frank Marcus (*The Killing of Sister George* starring a rampantly Sapphic Beryl Reid in the title role) but the core of the serious audience began to commit itself to the subsidized theatre, so much wider in its range and so much richer in talent across the board. The West End became the land that time forgot, graced with state visits from fading stars like Ingrid Bergman and Rex Harrison. Binkie Beaumont's last production, a disastrous staging of Joe Orton's *What the Butler Saw* (in 1969) starring West End stalwarts like Coral Browne, Stanley Baxter and Ralph Richardson – all of whom were booed to the echo on the first night – was a symbolic event, signalling Beaumont's loss of touch with his audience. His production represented an undignified scramble onto a bandwagon that had no place in the West End; had the play been staged at either the National, the RSC or the Royal Court at the same time, it would surely have been an enormous success. The managers and the public had lost confidence in one another, and the West End started to become, as it continues to be, a place to which to transfer exciting work, but not one in which to start it.

Snowdon's photographs of the period (he had been made Earl of Snowdon the year after his marriage to Princess Margaret) reflect these changes. They caught the new breed of actor: David Warner and Glenda Jackson at the RSC (the latter exceptional actress would scarcely, on either vocal or facial grounds, have scraped a living in previous generations) and Albert Finney, shown here daringly sockless, heir-apparent, it seemed, to Laurence Olivier. After a powerful *Luther* at the Royal Court and a sensational season at the National Theatre, he had been discovered by the movies, and seemed from that moment, despite a return to the National in the seventies and many subsequent appearances in the West End and at the Royal Court, to have lost his appetite for the sort of career that Olivier carved for himself. This was the first intimation of what would eventually become a crisis in the British theatre: the final demise of the actor-manager.

Here, too, is Peter Cook, one of the four prodigally gifted young men who created and starred in *Beyond the Fringe*, the revue that ended revues. As founder of the Establishment Club, he was a harbinger of the new satire movement of the sixties,

70s

joyfully demolishing what was left of the pompous self-satisfaction of the vestiges of Imperial attitudes: an impulse which would become the dominant mode of English humour for the next twenty-five years, long after the original targets had been blasted away. The photographs of Olivier and Joan Plowright at home in Brighton exactly express the new spirit of democracy and ease within the British theatre; the informality and warmth of these pictures form a striking contrast to the iconic portraits of Olivier and Vivien Leigh of ten years before. The mystery and separateness of actors was vanishing, too, with interesting consequences for acting styles in the coming decades.

The theatrical sixties ended with the first remarkable years of Trevor Nunn's control of the Royal Shakespeare Company. Appointed in 1968 by the departing Peter Hall, he was at twenty-eight years old an astonishingly mature director, and, in conjunction with the designer Christopher Morley, quickly established a style which, while not breaking entirely with Hall's text-centred approach or his conviction that culture embodied society's moral values, explored the issues of power and sex with a glistening sensuality which presaged the coming decade of strutting capitalism, and signalled a departure from the more overt political concerns and utopian yearnings of the sixties. Peter Brook's inspired production of *A Midsummer Night's Dream*, a miracle of creative imagination, and a complete reinvention of the terms of classical theatre, was, though technically it appeared in 1970, a farewell to the ideals and emancipations of the previous decade. Snowdon's photograph conveys the dizzying exhilaration of Sally Jacob's white box in which all the production's magic was worked; he has caught, too, the open sensuality of the lovers, in the comely forms of Mary Rutherford and Christopher Gable. (Brook, who had, fifteen years before, asked Snowdon to design *Irma La Douce* for him – Rolf Gerard did it instead – told him that the inspiration for the white box had come from the photographer's studio in Pimlico.)

Olivier's National Theatre was approaching its peak in that same year of 1970. Ingmar Bergman was invited to direct *Hedda Gabler*; the entire production epitomized the ideals on which the company had been based. Robert Stephens, Olivier's number two at the Old Vic, also at his peak, with his staggering performance as Atahuallpa in *Royal Hunt of the Sun* and a sexily funny Benedick behind him, played Løvberg; Maggie Smith played Hedda in one of the most restrained, most devastating performances of her career. The production had directly stemmed from the visit to the World Theatre Season of Bergman's Royal Dramatic Theatre production of the play. Peter Daubeny, who created the season in association with the RSC at the Aldwych somehow magicked the not inconsiderable sums involved in presenting, year in and year out, an annual season of the world's greatest companies, from the Kathakali Theatre of India, to the Japanese Noh Theatre, Eduardo de Filippo and Smoktunovsky, Wajda and Victor Garcia. It was an astonishing feast which directly influenced the work of British directors, designers and actors, and which gave audiences a glimpse of how rich and diverse the theatre might be. Daubeny died in the middle of the decade, and his dream died with him; the theatrical banquet disappeared, like Prospero's in *The Tempest*.

The mid seventies brought massive upheavals, politically and, as an inevitable consequence, theatrically. Margaret Thatcher became Prime Minister, and commenced the implementation of the programme on which she had been elected: the

revenge of the petite-bourgeoisie on a society – though she rejected the word – in which, as she saw it, decent, hard-working, God-fearing citizens were underwriting a vast number of non-contributory hangers-on. This inevitably included the beneficiaries of subsidy. It had seemed during the sixties that the arts budget, administered by the Arts Council, would continue quietly to expand. It might never reach the levels of European subsidy, but decent growth might be maintained. Thatcher's first administration swiftly provided a rude awakening from this daydream.

From now on, no one running a theatre could assume anything. A long period of retrenchment set in, although paradoxically a great physical expansion, the legacy of the optimistic sixties, was everywhere to be seen. The National Theatre left the Old Vic to occupy its new home on the South Bank, a building already aesthetically obsolete by the time it was constructed, and not in perfect running order for some years to come. It was, however, on an altogether larger scale than the Vic, with its three auditoria, its innumerable dressing rooms and its huge public areas, and represented a massive endorsement of the theatre and its importance to the nation. The West End, the Royal Court and the regional theatres quailed at the sheer numbers of technicians, actors and designers – not to mention members of the audience – that this theatropolis would siphon off. Their fears were not altogether misplaced.

Peter Hall, having left the RSC in 1968, and briefly served as Head of Productions at the Royal Opera House, replaced a reluctant but visibly ailing Laurence Olivier in 1973 as head of the National Theatre, with the task of seeing the company into the new building. Such Cox-and-Boxing at the top inevitably led to a certain homogeneity, and the sharp differences that existed between the RSC and the National Theatre at the Old Vic faded away. But Hall was the man for the job. It took all of his prodigious energies and administrative genius to make a success of what many continued to regard as an unnecessary behemoth (Jonathan Miller, for instance, having worked frequently and successfully as a director at the Old Vic under Olivier, resoundingly denounced both the new theatre and its director); but, in conjunction with a team of fellow directors including Bill Bryden and Christopher Morahan, he did it, constantly devising new ways of creating an identity for the company, at one time running three companies, each attached to one of the auditoria, at other times permutating actors across the theatres, and at yet other times simply assembling an ad hoc group to perform a particular play. Despite the presence in the company at various times of Ralph Richardson, John Gielgud, Paul Scofield, Robert Stephens and Albert Finney, there was no attempt to revive Hall's own earlier dream of an ensemble, except in the loosest sense; at times it appeared that the National Theatre had become H. M. Tennent on the South Bank. The public, however, rewarded by such sumptuous spectacles as *Amadeus*, quickly developed a loyalty – both to the building and to the company – which was comparable to that of the informed, intelligent West End audience of earlier decades. The West End itself, however, they increasingly deserted. Writers like Simon Gray and Alan Ayckbourn (mostly presented by Michael Codron) still flourished there, it was impossible any longer to rely on an audience of connoisseurs who would support an interesting if flawed play which had received less than universal praise. The alarming laws of the Broadway jungle began to operate, and unsuccessful plays could now close within weeks. Only safe and reliable work dared risk an outing; and increasingly that meant already acclaimed productions transferring from the subsidized sector.

The RSC was expanding, too, with new theatres at Stratford and London. The sort of sustained growth within the company which had characterized the early years of Peter Hall's directorship was gradually abandoned, though two-year cycles of work were established, with plays starting in Stratford and then playing in London; Trevor Nunn's dazzling Romans season assembled a remarkable group of players including Janet Suzman, John Wood and Richard Johnson, while Alan Howard, a key actor of the seventies, worked his way through the Plantagenet monarchs, completing his progress from a magnificent neurotic actor (Lussurioso in *The Revengers' Tragedy* and Achilles in *Troilus and Cressida*) to a heroic one under the direction of Terry Hands, who created an unmistakable look for many of his productions – leather overcoats, trousers and boots, a sort of fascist chic – which became an unofficial house style for the RSC.

The Royal Court, after a tremendous avant-garde explosion under an increasingly experimental Bill Gaskill, grew, under his successors, altogether more amiable, generating West End transfers for plays like Mary O'Malley's situation comedy, *Once a Catholic*. Gaskill himself, a great leader of theatrical fashion but a very poor follower of it, had created a touring company, Joint Stock, which was a paradigm of the proliferating groups of the seventies, most of which, like Gay Sweatshop and Red Ladder, had more or less explicitly political agendas. Joint Stock's purpose, from an essentially socialist position, was to find new forms of theatre by working with writers in new ways. One of the founders of Joint Stock, David Hare, who wrote the Maoist play *Fanshen* for them after a prolonged period of improvisation, was himself a director, and in 1978 Peter Hall invited him to stage Howard Brenton's *The Weapons of Happiness* at the National Theatre. This was the beginning of the assimilation of the work of the New Wave of British writers (essentially Royal Court writers) by the major subsidized theatres. Edward Bond shortly followed. These writers, led by Hare, became the backbone of those theatres' new writing. They spoke for England in a series of state-of-the-nation plays of increasing richness and sophistication, availing themselves of the full technical possibilities of the new theatres. Despite Hare's *Knuckle* at the Comedy Theatre (1974), most of these writers would never have received an airing in the West End; large in scale and public in nature, their plays were now in the mainstream, which is what the National Theatre and the RSC had become.

It is understandable that Snowdon, nephew of Oliver Messel, would not find himself drawn to the theatre of the seventies. In fact, he had become deeply involved in photographing and then later filming people as far removed from the theatre as could be, many of whom fell into Margaret Thatcher's category of the unproductive: the old, the disabled, the impaired. He never again photographed a whole production (though he did, for example, bring his camera to a run-through of *Amadeus*); but nor did he ever lose his fascination with theatre people as a breed, and his work with them over the subsequent decades is a formidable record of the profession which had, since his early days, changed out of all recognition.

Nicol Williamson, for example, is captured, thanks to one of those happy accidents so welcomed by Snowdon, in motion, and the consequent blur superbly expresses the Francis Baconish qualities that he brought to his work in this decade – alienation, neurosis, despair, disintegration. Alan Bates, altogether more

solid, though by no means lacking in ambiguity, proved an extraordinarily durable actor, having started his London career at the Royal Court in its first season (he created the role of Cliff in *Look Back in Anger*), was subsequently to be seen in Sloane Square, but, in a reversal of the trend, was more often to be found in the West End, one of the few stars able to command a following for the new work in which he has constantly appeared. It had become apparent by now that, despite excellent work from individuals, there was going to be no succession to the Olivier/Gielgud generation of great actors. The theatre, in becoming writer-centred, director-centred, or even designer-centred, had ceased to centre on actors, and there accordingly appeared a void which no single actor seemed willing to fill. Perhaps Olivier had created an act that was impossible to follow; perhaps the whole idea of Great Acting seemed redundant. Certainly it was hard to think of anyone who should by rights inherit the sword that Kean had used when he played Richard III and which Gielgud had ceremonially presented to Olivier after his overwhelming performance in the same role. Asked who would be the next actor to get it, Olivier had replied, 'No one. It's mine.' And no one did get it, nor perhaps, ever will again.

In another photograph from this decade Peter Brook, unrecognizably transformed from the puckish presiding genius of the West End of the fifties into a guru, trots across the rehearsal room with characteristic élan and economy of purpose; the production he was directing, however, *Antony and Cleopatra* with Glenda Jackson and Alan Howard, was not a happy one: it was his last production with the RSC and the last production of his to originate in Britain, another of the great absentees of the modern British stage.

The novelist David Storey created, during this decade, a body of work out of no tradition, owing nothing to anybody, performed at the Royal Court as long as Lindsay Anderson was working there; and the lyricist Tim Rice, photographed at the time of *Jesus Christ Superstar*, is central to that unprecedented revival of the British musical (many of them written by Andrew Lloyd Webber) without which half the theatres in London – indeed, half the theatres in the world – would now have closed.

The musical came increasingly to occupy the West End, bringing coachloads of people from all over the country, eager for physical excitement, spectacle and pounding, massively amplified rhythms: a new audience for a new form of theatre, a novel mixture of rock concert and Palladium spectacular. The production by Trevor Nunn of Lloyd Webber's *Cats* was a significant symptom of this new West End dominated by musicals, most of them staged by graduates, like himself and the designer John Napier, of the subsidized theatres. The eighties were notable for a blurring of the divisions between the commercial and the public sectors: *Les Miserables* originated at the RSC, but was clearly destined for the West End – was in fact largely paid for by a commercial producer, Cameron Mackintosh. Unloved by the critics, it was embraced by the public, but it is certain that they would not have flocked in such droves had the show not had the imprimatur of the Royal Shakespeare Company's name attached to it. Nunn and his colleagues had consciously committed themselves to the idea of a commercial production in the – richly confirmed – belief that they might be able to make some much-needed money for the company, always less well funded than the National. The company's move to the Barbican in the City of London, planned since the mid-sixties, had now finally taken place. When it did, it was into another building, like the National Theatre, which took so long to get into construction that it was already out of date by the time it was built; in the case of the Barbican, the backstage facilities were so unsatisfactory and the front of house so unwelcoming that the company eventually moved out for part of the year.

During this decade, the whole structure of the profession began to change; or, more precisely, changes that had started considerably earlier began to manifest themselves. The repertory theatres, starved of money from increasingly rate-capped local government authorities, began to close down or cut their losses, no longer maintaining companies as they once had, no longer able to take risks on new plays, no longer able indeed to contemplate doing plays with above a certain number of actors in the company, or more than one set. The larger repertory theatres, like Nottingham under Richard Eyre or Bristol under Richard Cotterell, had been run as National Theatres in miniature. Where now would young directors, actors and writers learn their trade? There was never any shortage of talent; but experience – the fibre-building process of trial and error – was in dangerously short supply. The major companies began to appear rather lightweight, as increasingly few star actors were prepared to commit themselves either to a company or to a West End run, preferring to wait for television or film work; as indeed did young thrusting talents. Excellent theatre continued to be produced at the major houses on a magnificent scale – *Nicholas Nickelby* at the RSC, *The Oresteia* at the NT – and the Old Vic experienced a brilliant final flourish of private patronage in a couple of highly enterprising seasons directed by Jonathan Miller and underwritten by 'Honest Ed' Mirvisch and his son, who had renovated Lilian Baylis's old theatre to its former nineteenth-century glory (in the process inadvertently banishing the memory of its twentieth-century triumphs). Despite these successes, it was no longer possible to see in-depth company acting of a sort which had been the ideal, and indeed the achievement, of both Olivier and Hall when they had founded the two organizations; the notion of the ensemble was dead.

Olivier himself died in 1989, and his memorial service at Westminster Abbey was an act of mourning, not just for one actor, however extraordinary, but for the whole idea of theatre that he had incarnated. He was survived, and is still survived, by his great partner and sometime rival, John Gielgud, who played his last stage role, in Hugh Whitemore's *The Best of Friends*, when he was over eighty; his enduring grace and wit continues to remind the present generation of a stylishness and a devotion to craft which has more or less vanished. Ralph Richardson, too, predeceased his old friend, with whom, latterly, he had formed – in Harold Pinter's *No Man's Land* and David Storey's *Home* – a sublime double act. His final incarnation during his last years as a sort of Zen master manqué appearing in but only slightly connected to a series of rather slight pieces, was an astonishing feature of the London theatre till the early 1980s, his survival a miracle, his presence a kind of anarchic blessing. Scofield, too, though vigorous and fairly regularly (though not regularly enough) to be seen on the stage, was an inspiring survival of another world of theatre: certainly the last actor of note to have made his living more or less exclusively on the stage. Maggie Smith is perhaps the only actor of our times to have had a career that in any way resembles the careers of her great predecessors – despite, or perhaps because of, her disappearance from the British stage in the seventies. Enraged by the negativity

of the London press, she withdrew to Canada, where, in Stratford, Ontario, she played all the great roles. That was London's loss; but the important thing is that she played those roles, and her development as an actor has followed a steady arc, till she is now at an absolute peak, her unique instrument perfectly at her command and at the service of whichever play she chooses to appear in, to which her audience will flock as long as she cares to perform it.

Anthony Hopkins, after long years in Hollywood, returned to the National Theatre in a blaze of glory, to act in David Hare and Howard Brenton's *Pravda*, then played in *Antony and Cleopatra* with Judi Dench (who has, like Maggie Smith, maintained an unwavering line of development in her theatre work); his subsequent appearance in *King Lear* was less happy, and after a London run in *M Butterfly* he returned to Hollywood to reach newer heights of fame on film. Virtually every actor of Hopkins' generation with the exceptions of Ian McKellen, Derek Jacobi and Michael Gambon, has seemed increasingly to shy away from the theatre, dropping in from time to time, as if, in Christopher Isherwood's famous phrase, merely down there on a visit. Among actors of the next generation, Tony Sher – also a brilliant novelist and dazzling painter – emerged as a classical star of the eighties, having spent most of his acting life in the subsidized theatre. His ability to transform himself (seen at its brilliant best in his *Richard III* for the RSC, a paraplegic Plantaganet fearsomely propelled by high-speed crutches) is the mark of a true bravura actor; in that sense he has inherited Laurence Olivier's mantle. Roger Rees, whose fine performance of the title role in *Nicholas Nickelby* took him to America, where he chose to stay, is an actor, and particularly was a Hamlet, very much in the *noble* tradition, but somehow slightly embarrassed by it, as if he knew that it was not right for the time. There has been an uncertainty of style in acting of the eighties and nineties, a dallying with rhetoric, and a loss of emotional contact, which is no doubt symptomatic of the time.

The phenomenon of the age is, without question, Kenneth Branagh, who has leapt from triumph to triumph, and from career to career, with an agility that makes the young Orson Welles look something of a slouch. Starring in the West End almost before he'd left RADA, he was immediately snapped up by the RSC to play Henry V; frustrated by what they were subsequently able to offer him, he founded with David Parfitt a company of his own (provocatively called Renaissance) which he took out on the road with his own production of *Romeo and Juliet* and a play he had himself written; he then created a touring Shakespearean company and engaged the services of three very distinguished Shakespearean actors – Judi Dench, Derek Jacobi and Geraldine McEwan (featured in Snowdon's group photograph) to direct the plays, in most of which he played the leading role; he brought them to London where they played a season for which it was impossible to get tickets; meanwhile he had re-directed his own stage production of *Twelfth Night* on film for television. The producer Stephen Evans urged him to direct and star in a film of *Henry V*, which he then did, to huge international acclaim; he next made films of *Much Ado About Nothing* and *Frankenstein*, throwing in a couple of other movies and a performance of the uncut *Hamlet* for the RSC, while masterminding a series of radio productions of Shakespeare, two of them starring John Gielgud.

This is an unprecedented career; there can be no useful comment on it, except to record that it has happened. Branagh is in love with acting, the theatre, and film to the bottom of

90s

his heart. He has turned a lot of people on to his loves who might otherwise have been indifferent to them. It is impossible to predict what new worlds he will need to conquer; but he will certainly be around for as long as any of these media exist.

The nineties have brought no great change, but an inexorable development down the same path. Subsidy seems more and more precarious since we have entered the Age of the Lottery, designed to be the salvation of the arts, but now turning into a double-edged sword: a possible threat to the government's commitment to the idea of state funding (let them get it from the lottery) and a source of public resentment: thanks to the incompetent handling of publicity, the impression has been given of massive handouts for elitist activities, while hospitals close for lack of funds. The drama schools, the source of the great, vaunted and internationally envied strength of British acting, are foundering for lack of funds, while students are no longer able to get awards from their financially crippled local authorities. The RSC has abandoned the Barbican for half the year in favour of more extensive touring, while the National, in splendid condition, enterprising and successful, after Richard Eyre's ten years' stewardship, is fighting to be allowed to make improvements in a building, never lovely to begin with, which has weathered badly.

The West End has flailed around, its empire long lost, its role still unclear, though it remains possible, with a Vanessa Redgrave or a Maggie Smith in the lead, to buck the trend and lure the audience away from the perceived superior comforts of the subsidized theatres – their parking spaces and their bookshops, their restaurants and their legroom. And if the West End has become a large network of receiving houses for shows originating elsewhere, so what? If it enables an excellent play like David Hare's *Skylight* to transfer from the National Theatre and be seen by five times as many people as could see it in the small Cottesloe auditorium, well, so much the better. One of the more surprising manifestations has been the association between the maverick but profoundly stage-struck producer Bill Kenwright with Peter Hall, that doyen of the four decades of theatre recorded by Snowdon's camera. His company, under Kenwright's aegis, fields a large number of all-star productions of classics ancient and modern; a slightly less plush reincarnation of the H. M. Tennent of the fifties. Hall, ever surprising, has just, in August of 1996, announced the establishment of a permanent repertory company at the Old Vic doing classics and modern plays; this he claims is his final flourish. A likely story.

Taken all in all, the range of work across the country remains remarkable, especially in the Fringe, which has never been part of Snowdon's brief. New acting talent constantly asserts itself, even if it is given little opportunity to train, to mature and to develop; more plays are being written then ever before, despite the woeful lack of outlets for them, and at least five per cent are very good (which means a lot of plays); new and ever younger directors appear, eager to do bold and ever odder things to plays; designers provide them with more and more sensational environments in which to work their wonders. There is little idealism, and fewer ideas, but life in the theatre goes on abundantly. A holding operation has been in progress, and things have been, against all the odds, well held. People are still smiling; people are actually still laughing. Snowdon has observed all this, and, in his latest portraits, has returned to an earlier manner of his, before the time of grainy surfaces and single light. He's decided to have fun, and so his extended fresco of the British theatre c. 1995 is a riot of allusion and gentle parody:

a homage, in fact, to the delicious witticisms and romantic languor purveyed in his uncle Oliver's work – gauzy, fantastic, beautiful, full of poetry and loneliness – with perhaps an affectionate nod in the direction of his friend Angus McBean, against whom it was necessary at the start of his career to rebel, but for whom he always had the warmest respect. These photographs don't merely record theatre, they *are* theatre.

He has noted that today the director is easily as glamorous as his actors and generally more so, and, accordingly, posed a pride of young directing lions flexing their muscles. His group of designers are wonderfully baroque. His writers, quite properly, he takes a little more seriously. Osborne in his final manifestation, a walking advertisement for Burberry's, incongruous and yet somehow absurdly touching, the grand old angry young man, still glaring; Alan Bennett, a Living National Treasure, photographed in the grounds of a castle belonging to one of his victims, her Majesty the Queen, whom he wickedly, if affectionately, satirized in *Single Spies*; Arthur Miller testifying to the truth that though there may be no second acts in American life, the third act is often marvellous if you stick around long enough to find out; Harold Pinter, a post-war classic, now in the nineties experiencing a fresh wave of inspiration, writing full-length plays again, having meanwhile acquired a new career as an actor in his own plays, revealing himself in *The Hothouse* to be a dazzling comic player, his perfect control just containing a real anarchy of spirit; and Alan Ayckbourn who in the seventies and eighties turned out play after play miraculously fusing comic machinery and compassionate observation. He has latterly developed more darkly, not quite so much in tune perhaps with the mood of the times, but he continues to plough his own furrow in Scarborough, heroically dedicated to the triple causes of new writing, ensemble acting and regional theatre.

It is, finally, the actors whom Snowdon loves: Nigel Hawthorne, quietly biding his distinguished career till the role of his life turns up, which he quietly seizes, and triumphs with absolutely in two media; Gambon, that great original, in perfect complicity with the photographer, proclaiming loudly, 'B-ll-cks to Great Acting,' while constantly committing it; Ustinov, unsmiling for once, giving a glimpse of the deeper man beneath the faces and the voices; Ralph Fiennes, roaring; Rufus Sewell with his dangerous, sexy, sardonic swagger; Fiona Shaw's sharp challenge; Helen Mirren, somehow not quite of our age, preparing, one can only hope, to come and be the great stage actress she tantalizingly promises to be once every ten years; Vanessa Redgrave, most poetic of actors, glimpsed in an Edwardian dream landscape; the iconically sexy Felicity Kendal; Stephen Fry's great brainy head breaking up just prior to his breaking down; Jonathan Pryce as Fagin momentarily suggesting Irving as Shylock (a hint perhaps to him).

For four decades, on and off, sometimes in the wings and sometimes out front, often in the studio and sometimes in the street, Snowdon has watched the theatre and the people who make it with teasing affection and admiration. The book covers a period of startling change, and the change, sometimes obliquely, is here to see in these pages; as are the changes, many of them initiated by him, in the style of theatre photography. The final image chose itself, summing up all Snowdon's love of the theatre: two great actors, having drunk to the lees from the cup of life, and fallen down in a gutter or two, elegantly ablaze over a cup of tea – reckless, stylish, unrepentant.

The book is full of that spirit.

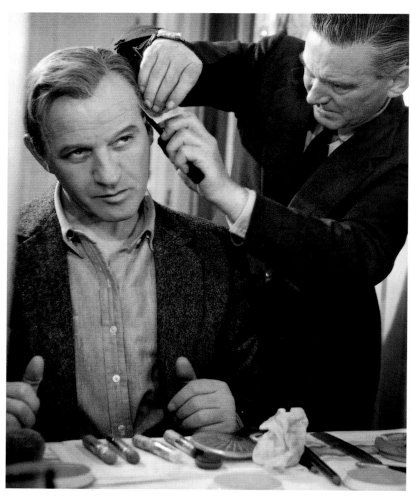

My first theatre photographs, published in 1954.
Margaret Leighton and Eric Portman played two parts
each, in *Separate Tables*, by Terence Rattigan,
directed by Peter Glenville, who was a great friend
of my uncle, Oliver Messel. It opened in Liverpool and
was a smash hit in London at the St James' Theatre

A double exposure of Margaret Leighton in the contrasting
roles of glamorous Mrs Shankland and spinster Miss Railton-Bell

OPPOSITE: Margaret Leighton and
Eric Portman making-up for their
respective roles, with Portman as
Mr Martin and Major Pollock

Margaret Leighton in Act I and Act II and, *below*, Eric Portman as Mr Martin.
I tried to get away from the formality of contemporary theatre photography, which was over-posed and heavily retouched

Barry Foster and Diana Churchill in *Desperate Hours*,
produced by Toby Rowland at the Hippodrome, 1955.
Toby gave me great encouragement and opportunities.
This was the first use of ten-foot enlargements outside
the theatre in place of the usual 10″ x 8″ glossies

Michael Redgrave in *Tiger at the Gates* by Giraudoux,
translated by Christopher Fry, directed by Harold Clurman,
at the Apollo Theatre, 1955. I was still taking very
stylized photographs with actors in heavy stage make-up

OPPOSITE: John Neville and Claire Bloom,
Romeo and Juliet, Stratford, 1956 – my first
photograph published in the *Daily Express*.
Posed with full stage make-up and thirties
studio spots, like a film still

Dirk Bogarde in *Summertime,* directed by Peter Hall, 1955.
I used a box of lights – twenty-five 100-watt bulbs in a large
contraption like a biscuit tin which fitted into the back of
my Morris Minor – to give the effect of a north light rather
than theatrical spotlights

Geraldine McEwan and Dirk Bogarde on Castle Hill,
Edinburgh, where *Summertime* was on tour.
They were in the mood of the play, which was
set in northern Italy, but was taken
outside to increase realism, rather than on stage

Alec Guinness as M. Boniface in *Hotel Paradiso* by Feydeau, translated and directed by Peter Glenville, 1956. OPPOSITE: This was taken during a rehearsal with a small camera and a normal lens. I just enlarged a small portion of the negative and bleached the eyes with potassium ferrocyanide. My first photograph to be published in *Vogue* under editor Audrey Withers. John Barber, the *Daily Express* theatre critic, unscrewed the photograph below from its display case outside the theatre and published it the next day in the *Express*. This upset the editor of the *Weekly Sketch* as I had already sold exclusive rights to him for £2!

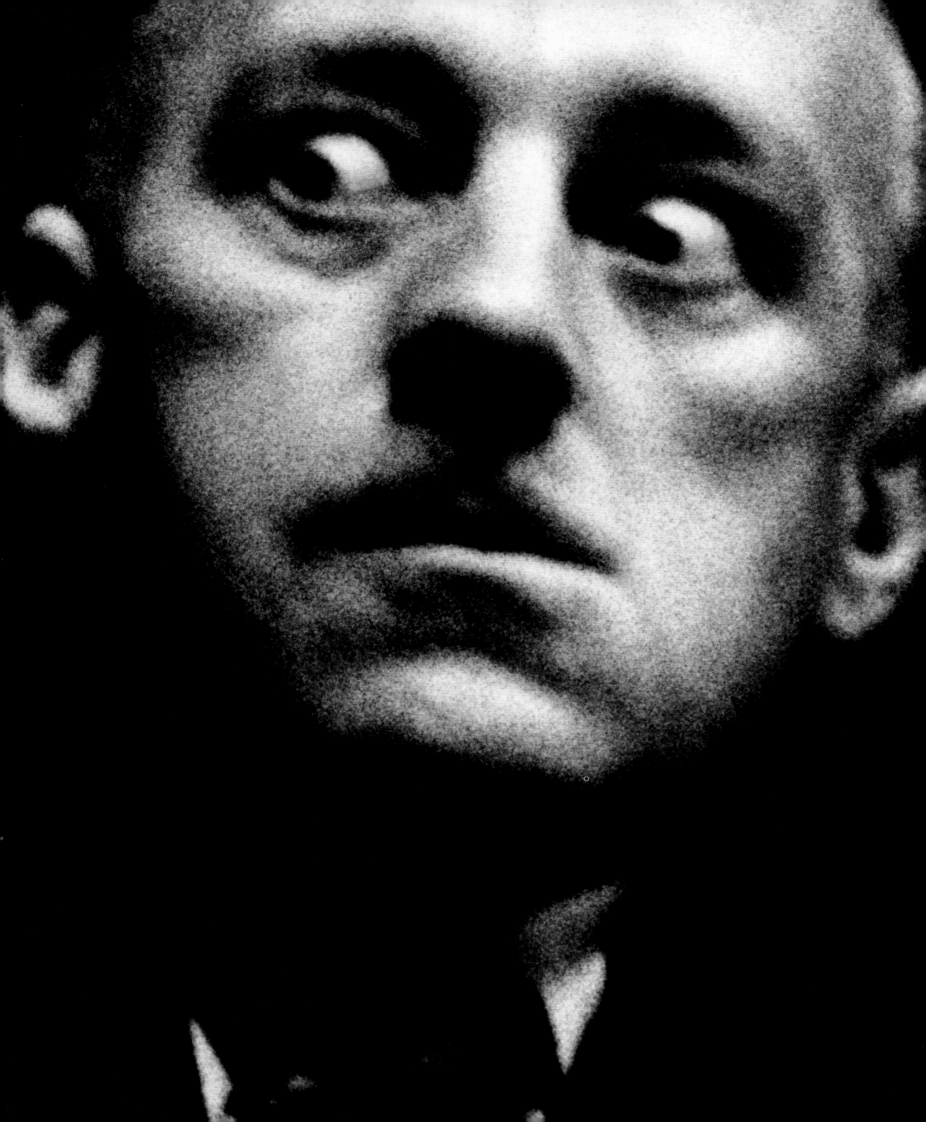

Paul Massie as Brick and Kim Stanley as Maggie in *Cat on a Hot Tin Roof* by Tennessee Williams, directed by Peter Hall, 1958. A more reportage-style photograph published in the *Daily Express*, whose features editor, Harold Keeble, started *Photonews* and encouraged young photographers to experiment. I was very lucky to have him as a patron

Laurence Olivier as Archie Rice
in *The Entertainer* by John Osborne,
directed by Tony Richardson at
the Royal Court, 1957. Taken from
the wings during a performance

Alfred Lunt in *The Visit* by Dürrenmatt,
directed by Peter Brook, 1957

Anthony Quayle and Brian Bedford in *A View from the Bridge*
by Arthur Miller, directed by Peter Brook, 1956. It featured
the first male kiss on stage, was banned by the Lord
Chamberlain, so was presented by a 'club' at the Comedy
Theatre where you paid 5/- membership at the door

Paul Scofield as the whiskey-priest in *The Power and the Glory*
by Graham Greene, directed by Peter Brook, 1956

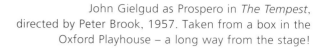

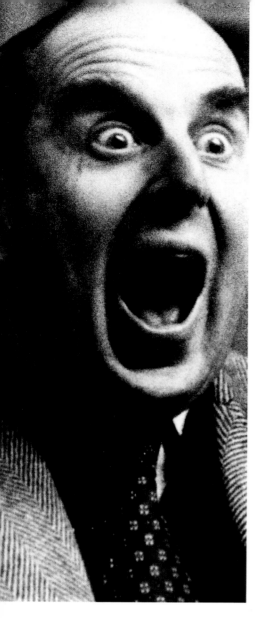

Robert Morley in *Fanny*, a musical of Pagnol's trilogy, *Vogue*, 1956

Edith Evans in *The Chalk Garden* by Enid Bagnold, directed John Gielgud, 1956

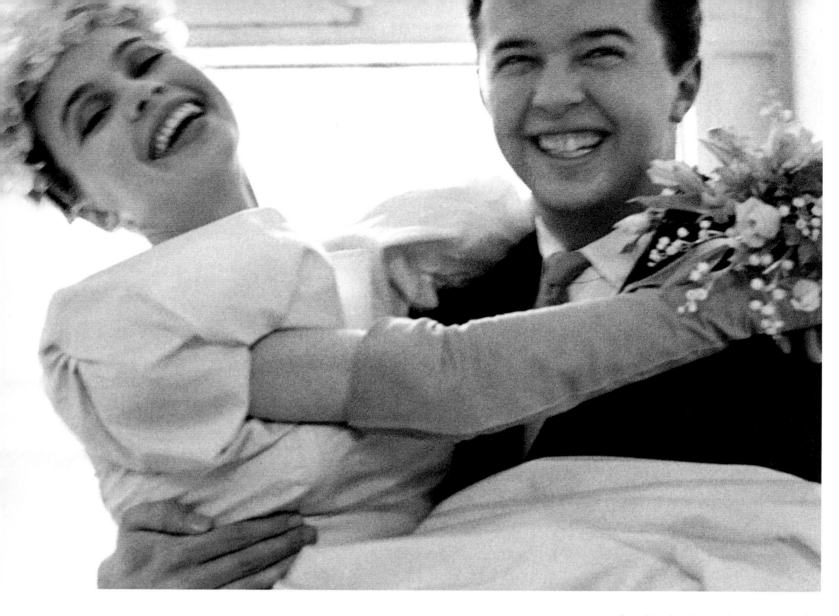

Peter Hall and Leslie Caron after their wedding
at Marylebone Town Hall, 1956. I was both
witness and photographer. Caron, *right*,
in Lerner and Loewe's *Gigi*, directed by Hall

Gladys Cooper, *The Crystal Heart*, 1957

Sybil Thorndike, *The Family Reunion* by T.S. Eliot, directed by Peter Brook, 1956

John Osborne, author
of *Look Back in Anger* and
The Entertainer, 1957

W. Somerset Maugham, author of *The Constant Wife*, 1958

AUTHORS FROM TOP: Jean Anouilh (*Ring Round the Moon*) 1957
John Arden (*Sergeant Musgrave's Dance*) 1958
Eugene Ionesco (*Les Chaises*) 1957

BELOW: Peter Shaffer (*The Royal Hunt of the Sun*) 1958

Brendan Behan, author of *The Quaire Fellow* and *The Hostage*, in a Dublin pub at 10am, 1957

T.S. Eliot lunching in Edinburgh
for the world preview of
The Elder Statesman, 1958

Dennis Potter, President of the University
Labour Club, Cowley, Oxford, 1959

Betty Marsden and choreographer John Cranko rehearsing
the musical *Keep your Hair On*, 1957. Desmond Healey designed the
costumes, John Addison composed the music and I designed
the sets. It was booed on the first night and closed after ten days!

Paul Robeson and Mary Ure, *Othello*, directed by
Tony Richardson, Stratford, 1959

Peggy Ashcroft rehearsing Margaret of Anjou for John Barton's
Shakespeare trilogy, *The War of the Roses*, Stratford, 1963

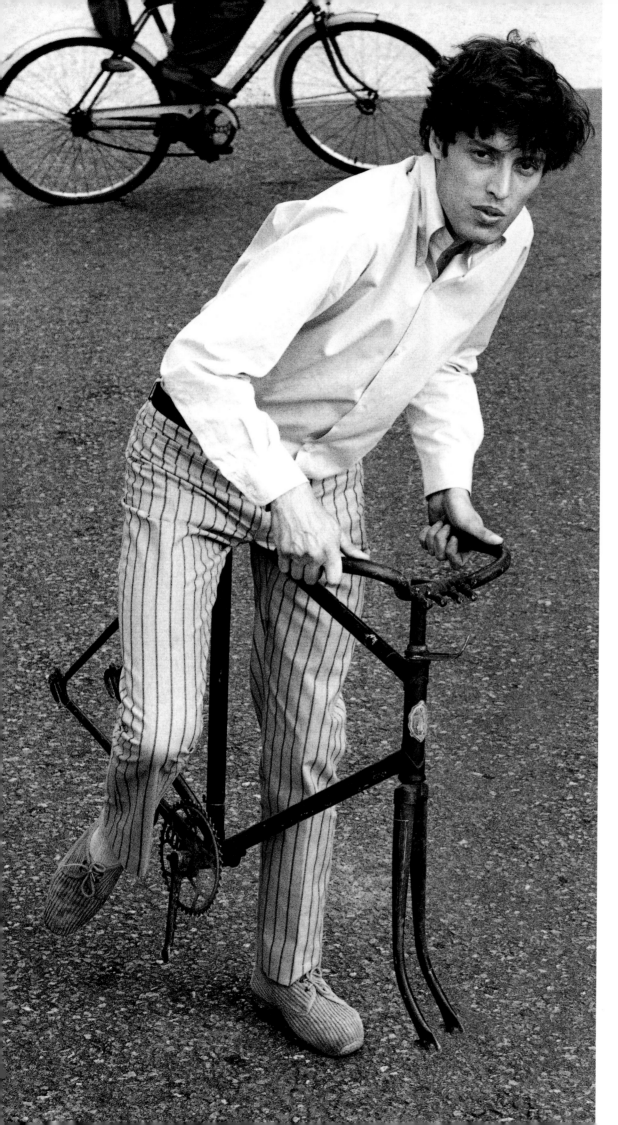

Noël Coward, Covent Garden, 1964

Tom Stoppard, Rotherhithe,
at the time of his play *Rosencrantz
and Guildenstern are Dead*, 1967

David Warner, *Hamlet*, 1965

James Hunter,
Ian Holm and
Roger Jones rehearsing
Edward IV,
The War of the Roses,
directed by
Clifford Williams,
Stratford, 1963

Diana Rigg as Adriana
with Donald Sinden as
Solinus, the Duke,
The Comedy of Errors,
Stratford, 1963

Roy Dotrice in the Green Room, Stratford during an interval. He was Caliban in *The Tempest*, 1963

OVERLEAF: Frederick Ashton and Robert Helpmann in the dressing room as the Ugly Sisters in *Cinderella*, choreographed by Ashton, Covent Garden 1965

Peter Cook, 1968

Albert Finney, 1960

LEFT: Laurence Olivier as Othello, 1962
TOP: Strindberg's *The Dance of Death*, 1967
ABOVE: Feydeau's *A Flea in Her Ear*, 1967
RIGHT: Chekhov's *Uncle Vanya*, 1962
FAR RIGHT: supper in Brighton with his wife, Joan Plowright, 1967

OVERLEAF: Dennis Waterman, *Saved*,
by Edward Bond, directed by
William Gaskill, the Royal Court, 1965

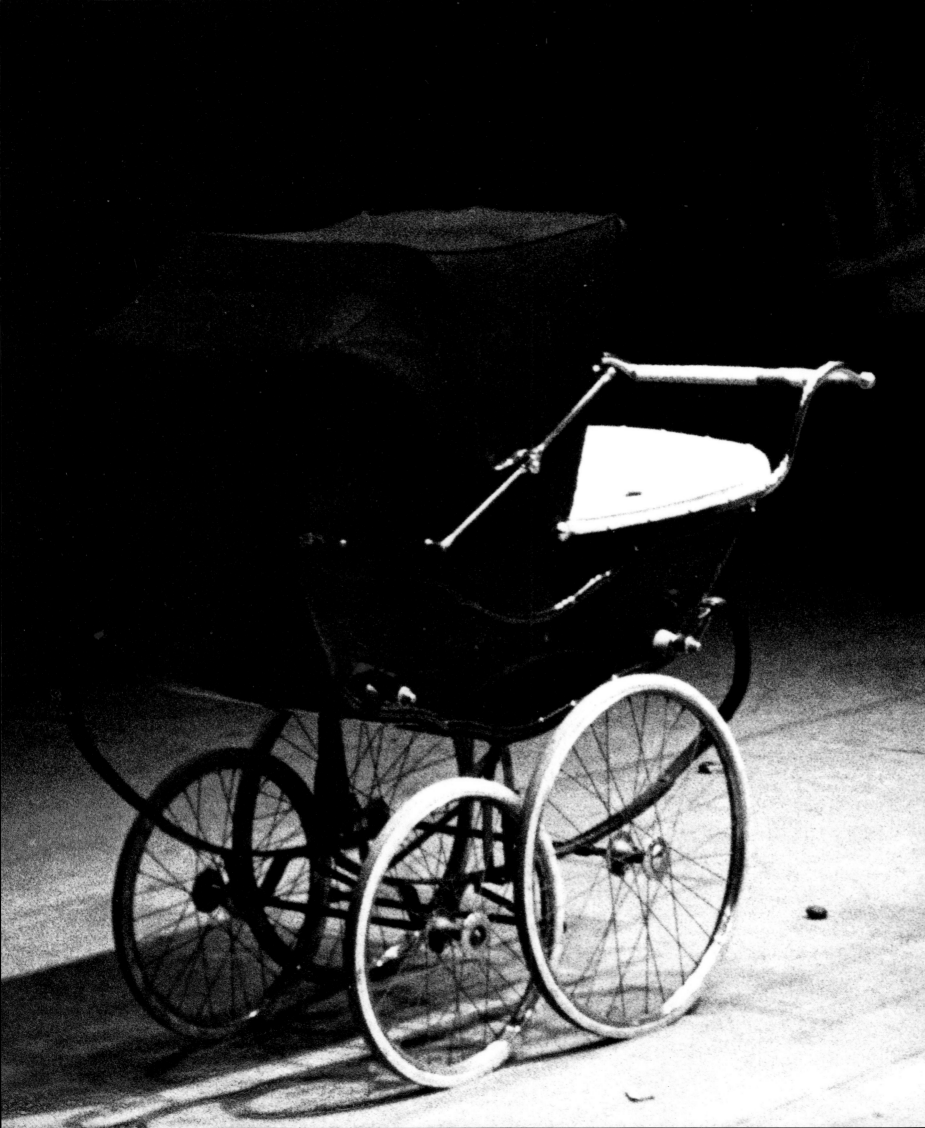

OPPOSITE: Glenda Jackson as Charlotte Corday and Sheila Grant, *above*,
as a madwoman in *Marat-Sade*, by Peter Weiss, directed by Peter Brook, 1966

Arnold Wesker, the Roundhouse,
converted to a theatre from a railway
engine-turning shed, 1962

George Devine, founder
and Artistic Director,
the Royal Court, 1962

Harold Pinter, author of
The Caretaker and
The Homecoming, 1968

Kenneth Tynan, critic,
(author of *Oh, Calcutta!*),
the National Theatre,
1963

Alec Guinness, *Wise Child*, by Simon Gray, directed by John Dexter, 1967

Eileen Atkins and Beryl Reid, *The Killing of Sister George*,
by Frank Marcus, directed by Val May, 1966

Michael Gambon and Penelope Wilton, *Betrayal*
by Harold Pinter, directed by Peter Hall, 1979

Felicity Kendal and Simon Callow rehearsing for *Amadeus*
by Peter Shaffer, directed by Peter Hall, 1979

Peter Ustinov, 1979

Jonathan Miller, 1978

Tim Rice, 1976

PRECEDING PAGES: *left*, Maggie Smith and Robert Stephens rehearsing Ibsen's *Hedda Gabler*, directed by Ingmar Bergman, 1970, *right*, Nicol Williamson as Bill Maitland in *Inadmissible Evidence* by John Osborne, the Royal Court, 1976

LEFT: Peter Brook directing *Antony and Cleopatra*, with Glenda Jackson and Alan Howard, Stratford, 1978

BELOW: Lindsay Anderson and David Storey, director and author of *This Sporting Life* and *The Changing-Room*, 1971

Christopher Gable and Mary Rutherford as
Lysander and Hermia, *A Midsummer Night's Dream*,
directed by Peter Brook, Stratford, 1970

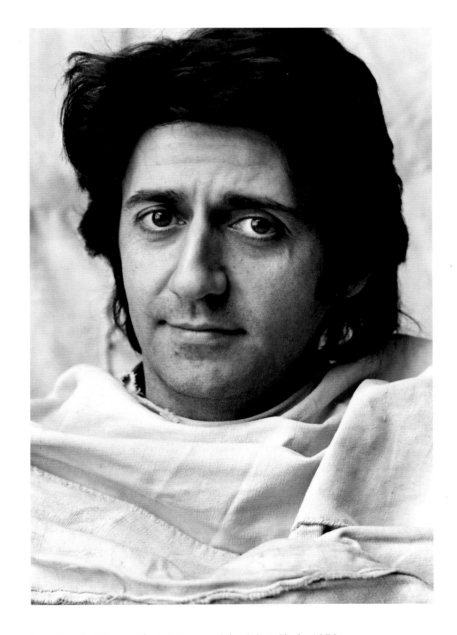

Tom Conti, *Whose Life is it Anyway?* by Brian Clark, 1979

Alan Bates, 1972

Edith Evans, 1977

Maria Aitken, 1978

Diana Quick, 1978

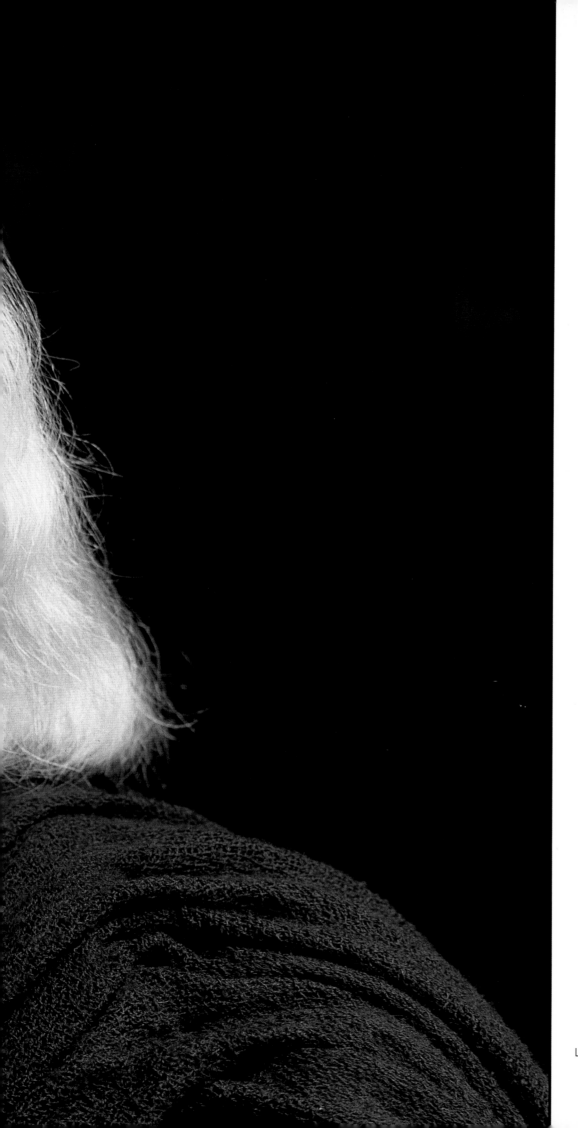

Laurence Olivier, *King Lear*, 1983

John Gielgud in his drawing room, 1988

Ralph Richardson, 1981

Paul Scofield, 1982

Trevor Howard and Cyril Cusack, *No Country for Old Men*, with director Tristram Powell, 1981

Alan Howard, *Richard II*, Stratford, 1980

Rik Mayall, 1983

Rowan Atkinson, 1986

Lindsay Anderson and Alan Bennett after their collaboration,
The Old Crowd, 1980

Graham Greene, 1988

Michael Frayn and Michael Rudman, 1980.
Rudman directed three of Frayn's plays: *Alphabetical Order*,
1975, *Donkey's Years*, 1976 and *Clouds*, 1978

Daniel Day-Lewis, *Hamlet*, directed by Richard Eyre,
the National Theatre, 1989

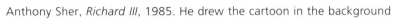

Anthony Sher, *Richard III*, 1985. He drew the cartoon in the background

Jeremy Irons, 1981

Renaissance Theatre Company: Derek Jacobi,
Judi Dench, Kenneth Branagh, Geraldine McEwan,
David Parfitt, the Phoenix Theatre, 1988

Roger Rees, *Nicholas Nickelby*, 1984

Richard E. Grant, 1988

Natasha Richardson, 1987

Sam Mendes, 1989

Kenneth Branagh on a sun-bed during rehearsal for *Othello*, in which he played Iago, 1995. Graydon Carter, editor of *Vanity Fair*, commissioned me to photograph the British theatre for a 56-page special issue from which many of the following pictures were taken

Derek Jacobi, *Hadrian the Seventh*, Chichester, 1995

Felicity Kendal, *Indian Ink* by Tom Stoppard, directed by Peter Wood, 1995

Michael Bryant, Badger, 1993

Adrian Scarborough, Mole, 1993

Howard Ward, Otter, 1993

David Ross, Rat, 1993

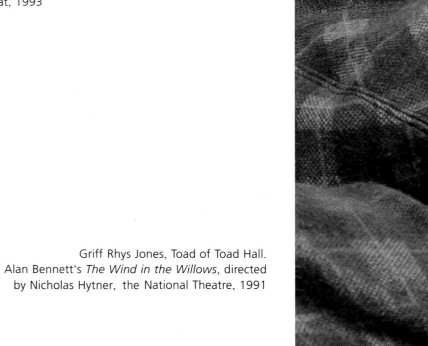

Griff Rhys Jones, Toad of Toad Hall.
Alan Bennett's *The Wind in the Willows*, directed
by Nicholas Hytner, the National Theatre, 1991

Christopher Hampton, 1995

Mike Leigh, 1996

Adrian Noble, artistic director of the
Royal Shakespeare Company, and Richard Eyre,
director of the Royal National Theatre.
The backdrop is for *La Grande Magia*, by
Eduardo de Filippo, 1995

Jude Law, *Indiscretions* by Jean Cocteau,
New York, 1995

Natasha Richardson, 1995

Designers, 1995: *left to right*,
Maria Bjornson, Ian MacNeil,
William Dudley, Stephen Brimson,
Jocelyn Herbert, Mark Thompson,
Carl Toms, Bob Crowley

Ian McKellen, 1991

Nigel Hawthorne, *The Madness of George III*
by Alan Bennett, directed by Nicholas Hytner, 1994

Alan Bennett. The Long Walk, Windsor, 1995. The 'Copper Horse' statue of George III is a reference to his play *The Madness of George III*, the butcher's bicycle a nod to his father's trade, and the corgis refer to his play *A Question of Betrayal* which portrayed the Queen and Anthony Blunt

Lionel Bart, composer of *Oliver!*, in Fournier Street where he was born

Jonathan Pryce as Fagin,
in *Oliver!*, 1994

Deborah Warner, director, 1995

John Sessions (by courtesy
of David), 1995

Alan Rickman on the Albert Memorial,
his favourite architectural monument, 1995

Zoe Wanamaker, the Globe Theatre.
Her father, Sam Wanamaker, dedicated
his life to its restoration, 1995

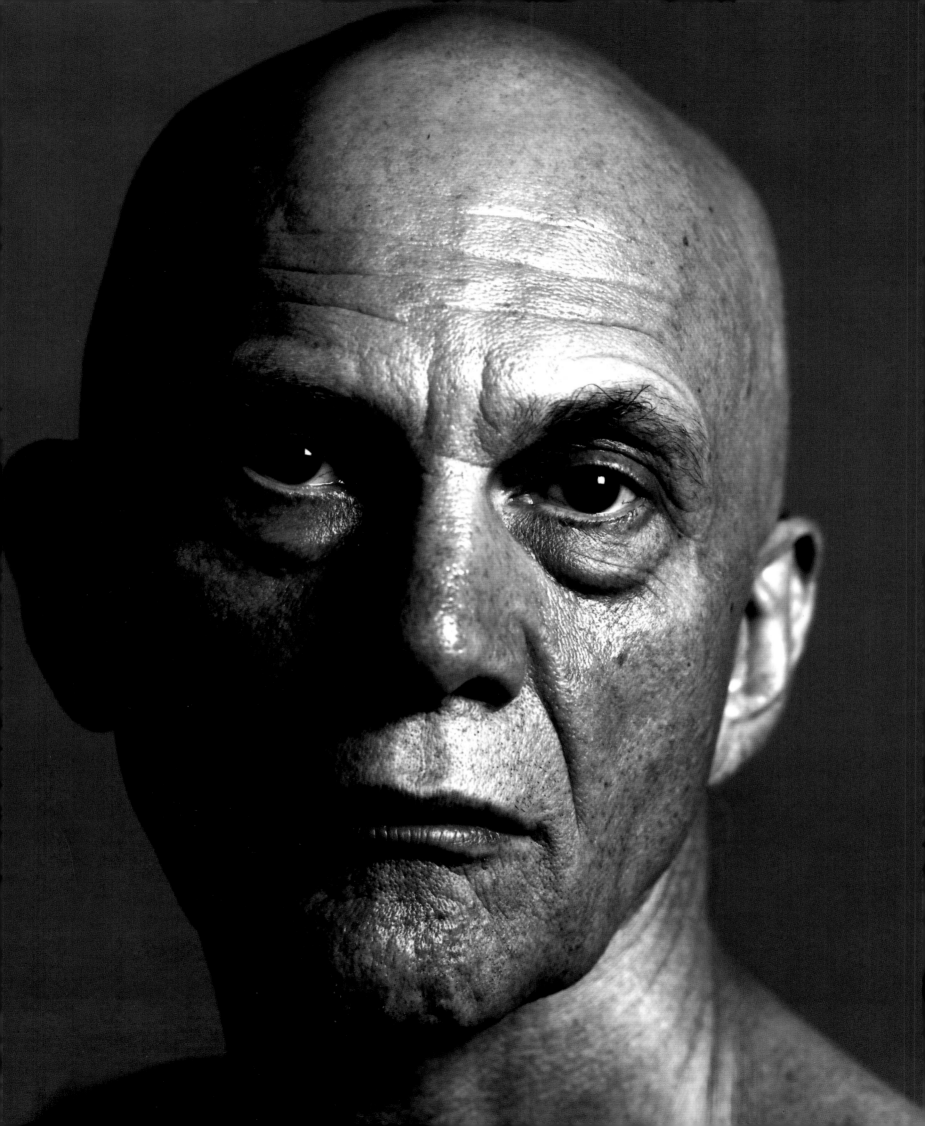

Ben Kingsley, 1995

Daniel Massey, *Taking Sides* by Ronald Harwood, 1995

Richard O'Brien, creator of *The Rocky Horror Show*, 1995

Helen Mirren, 1995

Ralph Fiennes, New York, 1995

Tom Courtenay, *Moscow Stations*, 1995

Julia Ormond, 1995

Juliette Caton, 1996

Jennifer Ehle, 1996

Emma Thompson (by courtesy of Velasquez!), 1992

132

Rupert Everett, 1995

Arthur Miller, The Salisbury, St Martin's Lane, 1991

John Osborne, 1991

Harold Pinter, author, director and performer
in *The Hothouse*, 1995

Steven Berkoff, 1995

Directors, 1995: *top*, *left to right*, Simon McBurney, Richard Olivier, Jonathan Kent,
bottom, *left to right*, Stephen Daldry, Roger Michell, Sean Mathias, Katie Mitchell, Sam Mendes, Matthew Warchus

Anna Massey as a Victorian nanny in Hyde Park
with my great-grandmother's pram, 1995

Alec McCowen and Penelope Wilton in
Ann Hathaway's apple orchard during the run of
Chekov's *The Cherry Orchard*, Stratford, 1995

Simon Callow in the mood of Monet, 1995

Juliet Stevenson
in my great-grandfather's
drawing room,
Punch cartoonist,
Linley Sambourne, 1995

Leo McKern,
Hobson's Choice by
Harold Brighouse,
Chichester, 1995

142

Rufus Sewell, 1995

Richard Wilson, 1993

Cats, 1995: producer Cameron Mackintosh, choreographer Gillian Lynne, composer Andrew Lloyd Webber, director Trevor Nunn, designer John Napier and the cast

Cameron Mackintosh, 1990

Nicholas Hytner, New York, 1995

Fiona Shaw as *Richard II*, directed by Deborah Warner at the National Theatre, 1995

Vanessa Redgrave narrating Kenneth Grahame's
The Wind in the Willows, Windsor, 1995

Patti Lupone, *Sunset Boulevard*, 1993

Miranda Richardson, 1995

Alan Ayckbourn, St John's Church, Wapping, 1995

Designer Nick Ormerod and director
Declan Donnellan, in Cheek by Jowl's production
of Webster's *The Duchess of Malfi*, 1995

Michael Gambon, Poets' Corner,
Westminster Abbey, 1995

Stephen Dillane with Ophelia and Yorick, *Hamlet*, 1995

Richard Harris and Peter O'Toole in the Oliver Messel Suite at the Dorchester, 1995

ACKNOWLEDGMENTS

I would like to thank all the actors, directors, producers, especially Binkie Beaumont and Toby Rowland, and backstage staff for giving so generously of their time and encouragement over forty-five years to take these these photographs: Peter Brook, Peter Hall, Peter Glenville, George Devine (and others at the Royal Court), Alec Guinness, Laurence Olivier, John Gielgud, Paul Scofield and the many actors who gave so me so much support in the 1950s.

I wish to express my gratitude to the many editors, writers and art directors who commissioned me, firstly Audrey Withers, editor of *Vogue*, who in 1953 gave me my first assignment, along with Harold Keeble, the legendary features editor at the *Daily Express,* John Barber, Beatrix Miller, Joan Juliet Buck, editor of French *Vogue*, Mark Boxer, Harold Evans, Nigel Horne, Drusilla Beyfus, Graydon Carter, Georgina Howell, Penelope Gilliat, Frances Wyndham, Michael Rand, Barney Wan, John Hind, Patrick Kinmonth, Alexandra Shulman, Lisa Lovatt-Smith, Isabella Kullmann, Susan White and Stephen Wood. My thanks also to Rosalind Chatto for endless vital information and John Humphries for his tireless support and enthusiasm since 1950.

I have been lucky to have had such wonderful assistants over the years: John Timbers, Robin Banks, Chris Drake, Derek Butler, Andrew MacPherson, Simon Mein, Alan Palmer, Richard Dudley-Smith, Tim O'Sullivan, Matthew Donaldson, Robin Matthews, John Cummings and, most recently, Graham Piggott, who has been quite exceptional in every way.

My warmest thanks go to Ray Watkins who art directed many of the recent sittings, found and chose the negatives from hundreds of cardboard boxes. She also designed the book with such patience, skill and graphic simplicity. I would also like to thank those who have run my studio: Heather Craufurd, Dorothy Everard, Sophie Miller, Kathy Baker, Evelyn Humphries, Lucy Manningham-Buller and Suzie Parry; Terry Lack for printing my black-and-white photographs, the team at Downtown, Paul Gatt at PushOne, and Terry Boxall for retouching. Others who have been a wonderful help in styling the 1995 photographs include Charlotte Pilcher, Maggie Hunt and Stephanie Spyrakis (make-up).

Lastly I would like to thank Simon Callow for contributing such an informative, personal and witty essay on the theatre.

SNOWDON

INDEX

Page references in *italics* indicate appearances in photographs